HAMPSHIRE IN PHOTOGRAPHS

MATTHEW PINNER

AMBERLEY

ACKNOWLEDGEMENTS

I would like to start by saying that I am entirely grateful to so many of the people who are close to me for supporting me while creating this book. First and most important is my beautiful wife, Emma: you have been my rock through this process and I love you very much. Also, my family: my mum, dad, brother and sister. Thank you for encouraging me after my first book and standing by me. My new family members, Ian, Debbie and Ben, for also believing in me and helping in any way when it comes to my photography.

There are also many members within the industry who have supported and guided me that I would like to give a special mention: Canon UK & Ireland, Angela Nicholson from *Camera Jabber*, Simon Parkin from *Somerset Weather*, Dean Murray from *Cover Images*, Corin Messer from *Bournemouth Echo*, Holly Green from *ITV Weather*, Elliot Wagland, John Challis, *Hampshire Life* magazine, Paul Vass, Gareth Richman and Elie Gordon from *BBC Earth*.

First published 2018

Amberley Publishing
The Hill, Stroud
Gloucestershire, GL5 4EP

www.amberley-books.com

Copyright © Matthew Pinner, 2018

The right of Matthew Pinner to be identified as the Author of this work has been asserted in accordance with the Copyrights, Designs and Patents Act 1988.

ISBN 978 1 4456 8203 7 (print)
ISBN 978 1 4456 8204 4 (ebook)

British Library Cataloguing in Publication Data.
A catalogue record for this book is available from the British Library.

Origination by Amberley Publishing.
Printed in the UK.

FOREWORD BY SIMON PARKIN

I've been very fortunate that I've been to some incredible places all over the world, thanks to my career. Now, obviously I always took my camera with me to capture the magic of the locations, but the results were at best passable and at worst terrible. But then I'm no Matt Pinner!

Matt doesn't just know what will make a great photo, he also has the natural talent to bring out the best in every picture he takes; the view, the composition, the lighting, he just instinctively knows how to get it right. Matt has that rare gift to take pictures of places that make the viewer feel as if they're almost there too.

INTRODUCTION

I first became interested in photography after my grandfather sadly passed away and left his tripod in his will for me. I found the inspiration from there, and have never looked back. I live by saying that you miss every shot you don't take. In any moment I have a chance. I'm constantly researching the next place to capture with my camera and when I'm free to explore I'm roaming around the UK's southern coast to capture as many images as I possibly can.

All the images within this book have been largely collected over the last year. While taking these images I explored as much of the county of Hampshire as I possibly could, so I have chosen the ones that mean something to me.

I love photography so much and I enjoy sharing the magical views I see in the early hours and last minutes of the day. I hope you enjoy the book as much as I enjoyed creating it.

ABOUT THE PHOTOGRAPHER

Matthew Pinner was born and raised for the early part of his life in the city of Southampton, Hampshire. After deciding at the age of twenty-two that he wanted to take up photography, he purchased his first camera after being left a tripod by his grandfather. It was his mission to learn everything he could by himself.

Matt's gallery of work is constantly expanding, along with the requests for a book of his work. The inspiration behind this book is to show the pure beauty of the county of Hampshire, which has been a massive part of his childhood. His large social media following, which reaches nearly 200,000 people, is also a constant source of inspiration for him.

Matt has achieved so much over the course of his five-year photography career, and many major TV outlets, newspapers and magazines have regularly asked to use his spectacular images to best represent the UK landscapes.

While on his photography outings Matt uses a Canon 5D Mark IV with a range of lenses by Canon. He uses a wide range of filters by Cokin.

Website: http://pinners-photography.co.uk
Facebook: Pinner's Photography
Twitter: @Matt_Pinner
Instagram: @Matt_Pinner
Email: enquiriespinnersphotogrpahy@gmail.co.uk

SPRING

Lone tree in South Downs, near East Meon

Longstock, near Winchester

New Forest, near Homesley

Calshot, Southampton

Calshot, Southampton

Chawton House Church

Andrews Mare

Mogshade Pond

Somerley House

Burley Manor

Micheldever Wood

Langstone Mill

Basingstoke Canal

Avington Country Park

Mogshade Pond

Mogshade Pond

Beaulieu Lake

Calshot, Southampton

Watercress Line, near Winchester

Watercress Line, near Winchester

St John's Church, Farley Chamberlayne

St Hubert's Church, Idsworth

Hatchet Pond

Andrews Mare

Milford-on-Sea

Cottage near Old Alresford

Hayling Island

Portsmouth

Longstock, near Winchester

SUMMER

Hinton, near New Milton

Hurst Castle

Hurst Castle

Rapeseed field, near Old Alresford

Lonely Tree, New Forest

Hinton Ampner, near New Alresford

Hinton Ampner, near New Alresford

Longstock, near Winchester

Emery Down, Lyndhurst

Hatchet Pond

Hatchet Pond

Rockford Common

Rockford Common

Exbury Gardens

Exbury Gardens

Lonely Tree, New Forest

Longwood Estate

Lepe Beach

Hayling Island

Keyhaven

Rockford Common

Lonely Tree, New Forest

Bursledon Windmill

Calshot, Southampton

St Hubert's Church, Idsworth

New Forest, near Bolderwood

St Mary the Virgin Church, near Old Alresford

Bolderwood Forest

Gate House, near Brockenhurst

Mayflower Park,
Southampton

Southampton Harbour Hotel

Southampton Dock

Lepe Beach

Exbury Gardens

AUTUMN

New Forest, near Rhinefield

Eling Tide Mill

Eling Tide Mill

Milford-on-Sea

Lepe Beach

Mottisfont

All Saints', Minstead

Milford-on-Sea

Milford-on-Sea

Ashlett Creek Tide Mill

Bursledon Windmill

New Forest, near Rhinefield

New Forest, near Rhinefield

Mogshade Pond

St Hubert's Church, Idsworth

Petersfield Lake

Petersfield Lake

Bolderwood Forest

Winchester Cathedral

Lòne Tree, near Rockford Common

Ashlett Creek Tide Mill

Hillier Gardens, near Winchester

St Leonard's, Hartley Mauditt

Andrews Mare

Lepe Beach

Hatchet Pond

Lepe Beach

All Saints', Minstead

New Forest, near Rhinefield

The Warrior, Portsmouth

WINTER

Rhinefield House

Rhinefield Forest

Rhinefield Forest

New Forest, near Homesley

Lone Tree, Mogshade Pond

Milford-on-Sea

Milford-on-Sea

Mogshade Pond

Lyndhurst High Street

Farley Mount

Emery Down Church

Longstock, near Winchester

Bursledon Windmill

Rhinefield Forest

Rhinefield House

Lepe Beach

Bolderwood Forest

Mogshade Pond

Mogshade Pond

Bolderwood Forest

Bridge in the New Forest

Rockford Common

Rhinefield House

Milford-on-Sea

Bursledon Windmill

Bridge in the New Forest

Longstock, near Winchester

Hatchet Pond

Somerley House